Listening To God

How We Can Have Pure Hearts and Be Blessed

Glenda Fulton Davis

WestBow Press books may be ordered through booksellers or by contacting:

WestBow Press
A Division of Thomas Nelson & Zondervan
1663 Liberty Drive
Bloomington, IN 47403
www.westbowpress.com
1 (844) 714-3454

Originally edited by Dr. John Sproule
Devotional art by Patricia Richardson Mattozzi

ISBN: 978-1-6642-0932-9 (sc)
ISBN: 978-1-6642-1339-5 (hc)
ISBN: 978-1-6642-0933-6 (e)

Library of Congress Control Number: 2020920168

Print information available on the last page.

WestBow Press rev. date: 02/05/2021

WESTBOW
PRESS®
A DIVISION OF THOMAS NELSON
& ZONDERVAN

Listening To God

How We Can Have Pure Hearts and Be Blessed

―――――――――

Bible study, devotions and prayers by
Glenda Fulton Davis

Seek and you will find.

Why We Study The Bible

Your word is a lamp for my feet, a light on my path.
Psalm: 119:105

For thousands of years, the Bible has been the standard for good behavior in all civilized societies. It is the definitive word on what is good and what is evil. Its principles are the foundation of freedom and liberty for all the nations that embrace its teachings.

The Ten Commandments were the original Old Testament laws of God. These laws were spoken by God, written on tablets, and given to the Jewish people to live by. These laws teach us to honor God and to respect the rights of others. They set boundaries and protect us from those who would harm us, and they keep us from bringing harm to ourselves and others. These laws were given by a loving God who wanted to help his people.

In the New Testament, Jesus explains his Father's words in a way that only he could. Jesus Christ, the Son of God, the Messiah, the Savior, the Redeemer of mankind, said he did not come to destroy the law, but he came to fulfill it. (Matthew 5:17).

This book brings to you some of Christ's wonderful teachings, and some practical ways that you can apply them to everyday living. Of course, we could not bring all of the words of Christ to you in this little book, but we have touched on some very important ones. God reveals all truth to us through his big book, the Bible. Our prayer is that God will reveal Christ to you through this little book.

"But seek first his kingdom and his righteousness, and all these things will be given to you as well."
Matthew 6:33

Seek God Early

**For the LORD is good and his love endures forever;
his faithfulness continues through all generations.**
Psalm 100:5

Life seems to be changing more and more every day, but God never changes. He is the same today as he was yesterday and as he will be tomorrow. He is always good, his words are always true, and he always keeps his promises.

Every day that begins with God is a good day. When you wake up each morning, think about God first. Thank him for giving you a new day and a new chance to do what is right. Ask him to help you learn good things and make wise choices. God has a wonderful plan for your life, and there is much that you need to know. Spend some time learning good things every day. It will help you to be wise when you are grown.

Thank you God for this new day.

Jesus replied: " 'Love the Lord your God with all your heart and with all your soul and with all your mind.'..."
Matthew 22:37

Love God

In fact, this is love for God: to keep his commands. And his commands are not burdensome...
I John 5:3

God is very great and very good. His ways are better than our ways. We should love and honor him.

How can we show our love to God? How can we honor him? There are many ways.

We can go to Sunday school and church to learn about God. We can study the life and teachings of his Son, Jesus, who was and is the image of his heavenly Father. We can sing songs of praise to worship him. We can spend time thinking about his goodness and mercy. We can pray and seek his will for our lives. These are just a few of the things we can do to show that we love him.

What is the best thing we can do to show our love for God? We can listen to him and do what he tells us to do.

Listen to Jesus Christ in this devotional. He speaks the words God. Listening to Jesus and obeying him will help you to have a pure heart and be blessed.

Heavenly Father, help us all to listen and learn from your Son.

'Love your neighbor as yourself."
Matthew 22:39b

Love Your Neighbor

Be kind and compassionate to one another...
Ephesians 4:32a

———

In addition to loving God best and putting him first, we should also love those around us. We should show love to each other by being kind. We should be kind at home, at church, at work, at school, and in our communities. But what is kindness, and how can we be kind?

Kindness means caring about the needs of others. Kind people are helpful, positive, and generous in their actions. They take responsibility. They become heroes to those around them.

Kind people are considerate and tactful. They know that words are important, so they try to choose their words carefully. Yet they are not easily angered by the thoughtless words of others. Kind people show a Godly type of grace to those around them.

If we want our neighbors to be kind to us, we must show kindness to them. If we want our neighbors to treat us with respect, we must treat them with respect.

Dear God, thank you for the people who have been kind to us.

"Blessed are the poor in spirit, for theirs
is the kingdom of heaven."
Matthew 5:3

Have Patience

Love is patient...
I Corinthians 13:4a

The Bible teaches us that God is patient. God sets a good example for his people to follow. We should try to be patient, also.

Patience means waiting for something. Anger, bad attitudes, and destructive behavior will not help us to live the way God wants us to live. Even if we have to wait a long time, we should still try to stay calm and be patient.

God does not want people to be mean, pushy or harmful to each other. He wants his children to keep sinful human spirits under control. He wants us to be controlled by his Holy Spirit. He wants us to treat other people the way we would want them to treat us.

Try not to get mad at people when you have to wait in long lines. Have patience. Other people have needs too.

Try not to become angry with yourself when you can't do something the first time. You will learn, if you patiently try to do things the right way.

Thank you, God, for the times you have been patient with us.

Jesus answered, "Unless I wash you, you have no part with me."
John 13:8b

Be Honest

If we confess our sins, he is faithful and just and will forgive us our sins and purify us from all unrighteousness.

I John 1:9

God the Father sent his only son, Jesus, to save the world from sin. Jesus died for sinners. Jesus can save, forgive, and make people clean inside. But people will not come to Jesus, unless they are honest about sin.

Some people refuse to admit their wrongdoing. They try to hide their sin or blame others.

God wants people to be honest. Hiding sin will not make it go away. Blaming others for your sin will only add more sin and cause unnecessary pain to others.

When you do something wrong, be honest and admit what you have done. Ask God to forgive you. If you have asked Jesus into your heart, God will forgive you. Honesty and prayer are necessary to have a pure heart and peace with God.

Dear God, thank you for teaching us to be honest with you, ourselves, and others.

"Ask and it will be given to you; seek and you will find; knock and the door will be opened to you."

Matthew 7:7

Pray

Humble yourselves before the Lord, and he will lift you up.
James 4:10

Whaen Jesus died on the cross, the veil of the Temple was torn apart. Now we can pray directly to God because of Jesus.

Some people think they can only pray in a building or temple. The truth is, we can talk to God anywhere. We can pray in the park, at home, at school, at work, at the beach, or any other place we happen to be.

We can pray anytime. We can pray morning, noon, evening or in the middle of the night.

We can pray in different ways. We can pray with our eyes opened or closed. We can pray out loud or quietly. We can sing praise songs to God, or we can just talk to God honestly from our hearts.

We can pray in different positions. We can pray on our knees or standing up or sitting down. If we are sick, we can pray propped up or flat on our beds. No one and no thing can keep us from praying.

God loves us. He wants his children to come to him and ask for what they need. He wants to help us, bless us, and give us his peace.

Heavenly Father, thank you for loving us and hearing our prayers. Your kingdom come, your will be done. In the name of Jesus, we pray.

"Blessed are those who mourn, for they will be comforted."
Matthew 5:4

Comfort Others

"And I will ask the Father, and he will give you another advocate to help you and be with you forever—"
John 14:16

When Jesus had finished his work on earth, he went back to heaven to prepare a place for us. Jesus did not want us to be alone. He asked his Father to send the Holy Spirit to be with us.

We are born again by this Spirit of goodness, truth and love that lives all real believers. The Holy Spirit helps us to gain wisdom and understanding. He reminds us of the words of God. He glorifies the Son. At times he prays for us. At other times he comforts us.

The Holy Spirit is a gift but he also gives gifts. Christians are given different gifts. God uses these gifts to help his church. These gifts enlighten, encourage, and comfort his people. The Spiritual gifts are listed in several places in our Bible. One place you can find them is in Romans 12:6-8.

Thank you, God, for giving wise counsel and comfort to us.

"Have faith in God,"
Jesus answered.
Mark 11:22

Have Faith

**Now faith is confidence in what we hope for and
assurance about what we do not see.**
Hebrews 11:1

Faith is believing in God, the Bible, and God's atoning work. Those
who are believers, learn to trust God and do things his way.

We cannot get to heaven by our own efforts, but by faith in the one
who loved us and gave himself for us. We are God's children, not by
physical birth but by a Spiritual rebirth.

God loves people. That is why he sent his only begotten Son, Jesus,
to seek and save those who were lost. We are made right with God by
believing in Jesus. Jesus is the atoning sacrifice for our sins.

We can trust God to do what he says in the Bible. We can believe
that he loves us. We can believe that he saves us for Jesus' sake. We can
believe that he hears our prayers. We can believe that he will be strong
when we are weak. We can trust him to help us, guide us, meet our
needs and protect us eternally. We can trust God to keep his promises.

Dear God, give people faith to trust in you and your way of salvation.

"**Blessed are the meek, for they will inherit the earth.**"
Matthew 5:5

Listen To the Shepherd

**The Lord is my shepherd, I lack nothing. He makes me lie down in green pastures,
he leads me beside quiet waters, he refreshes my soul. He guides me along the right paths
for his name's sake.**
Psalm 23:1-3

Sheep are basically tame, meek, humble animals who depend on their shepherd for guidance and protection. Lambs are baby sheep; they are the most vulnerable and needy of all the sheep.

Wolves are wild, predatory animals that attack the sheep. Unsheltered and unprotected sheep, especially lambs, are easy meals for hungry wolves.

A good shepherd is one who is willing to give his life to protect his sheep. Smart sheep learn to trust the good shepherd. If sheep ignore the shepherd's directions, they put themselves and their young ones in danger.

A good shepherd wants what is best for his sheep. He watches. He prays. He calls to those who stray. If necessary, he will leave the sheepfold to find his lost lambs. He forgives. He restores. He guides his sheep away from danger to places where they can be safe and grow strong.

Good Shepherd, help people to hear your voice.

"Blessed are those who hunger and thirst for righteousness, for they will be filled."
Matthew 5:6

Be Thankful

Give thanks to the Lord, for he is good; his love endures forever.

Psalm 107:1

When someone gives you a gift, it is polite to say, "Thank you." That is what we do when we pray before we eat. We thank God for the gift of food. Thanking God reminds us that God loves us, and he has given us the things we need to live.

It is true that your parents, grandparents, or others purchase the food and prepare it. But it first came from God. God is the one who put life in the seeds. He made the earth, the sun, and the rain so the plants would grow and become food for us.

Are there some other things for which we should be thankful? What about those who take care of you, protect you from harm, and teach you good things like the verses in this book.

If we take time to think about it, we will find that we all have many blessings in our lives for which we should be thankful. Thank God for your good friends, your favorite teacher, your pet, and all the beautiful things in nature. And don't forget to thank God for Jesus, the most special gift of all.

Thank you, God, for all the blessings you give to your children.

"Blessed are the merciful, for they will be shown mercy."
Matthew 5:7

Show Godly Mercy

Mercy triumphs over judgement.
James 2:13b

——◆▶

Jesus did not like the judgemental and proud attitudes of some of the religious leaders of his day. They talked about being God's children, but they were not his spiritual children. They did not have God's discernment, wisdom, power, or love.

Jesus was the Son of God by birth and Spirit, but he humbled himself. He came to obey the will of his Heavenly Father and to save people. It was the love, respect and mercy that Jesus showed that won the respect of the people around him. If we are to have good relationships with people, we need to have the same attitude as Jesus.

Like Jesus we should love people, even when they do not act loveable. We must forgive people, even when we do not think they deserve our forgiveness. We should do this in obedience to our Heavenly Father. Our joy will come from knowing that we are doing God's will and he will reward us.

We are all at different stages of Christian growth. We must all stay humble and treat each other with respect. Humble, understanding, and helpful people will be the ones who are loved and respected the most.

Thank you, God, for showing mercy to us.

"Blessed are the peacemakers,
for they will be called children of God."
Matthew 5:9

Seek Peace

Peacemakers who sow in peace reap a harvest of righteousness.

James 3:18

God made the world and all the things in it. He cares about everything that he made, but most of all God cares about people. He cares about all the people of the world.

Every person on earth is different. We do not look, act or think alike. If people are not careful, these differences can cause them to fuss and fight with each other.

All people were made by God. We should respect what God has made. We should be considerate and kind. We should be respectful, even when we disagree.

The best way to make peace is to share good things with others. Caring about the needs of others shows God's love. When people know you care about them, they will be much more interested in what you have to say.

Be kind. Be helpful. Be generous with others. Sow peace in a Godly way, and be patient while your seeds take root.

Dear God, help people to know your peace.

"Blessed are those who are persecuted because of righteousness,
for theirs is the kingdom of heaven."
Matthew 5:10

"Blessed are you when people insult you, persecute you and falsely say all kinds of evil against you because of me. Rejoice and be glad, because great is your reward in heaven,"
Matthew 5:11-12a

Forgive Your Enemies

Jesus said, "Father, forgive them, for they do not know what they are doing."
Luke 23:34a

Have you ever been unfairly picked on by others? Sometimes this happens to Christians. If this happens to you, try to stay away from the hurtful person. If this is not possible and you are afraid, tell someone you trust. Don't deal with it yourself. A godly person will protect you.

After the problem is corrected, what can we do to get rid of the bitterness and anger that may still be in our hearts? In Matthew 5:43-48 of the Bible, Jesus tells us to love and pray for our enemies. This may seem like a strange thing to do, but this is what Jesus did.

Jesus was lied about, laughed at, spit on, beaten, and put on a cross to die. What did Jesus do? He asked his Father to forgive those who were persecuting him. Jesus wanted to save people, even those who were mean to him.

We can overcome evil with good by praying for those who have hurt us. Our prayers can make a change in their hearts. It can also make a change in ours.

Praying for our enemies helps us to forgive them. Doing good, instead of getting revenge, shows a Christ like love which is a witness to them. If we can forgive everyone, even our enemies, it will help us to have a pure heart and peace with God.

Heavenly Father, thank you for sending Jesus to be our Savior and Lord. And Jesus, thank you for showing us how we can forgive others.

"By this everyone will know that you are my disciples, if
you love one another."
John 13:35

Show Love

Love does not delight in evil but rejoices with the truth. It always protects, always trusts, always hopes, always perseveres.
I Corinthians 13:6-7

Anyone can say, "I love you." How do we know if it is true? We know by what the person does.

If someone really loves you, they want what is best for you. This may not always be what we want, but it will always be what is right and good.

Parents show their children that they love them by protecting them from harm and by providing the things their children need to grow healthy and strong. They try to set a good example for their children to follow. And they teach their children good things, like the things in this book.

How can children show their parents that they love them? They can obey their parents the first time they are told to do something. They can try to get along with their brothers and sisters. They can be thankful and respectful.

We all need to feel loved. The best way to get love is to give Godly love to each other.

Dear God, thank you for the love of family.

"My command is this: Love each other as I have loved you."
John 15:12

Be A Helper

Therefore, as we have opportunity, let us do good to all people, especially to those who belong to the family of believers.

Galatians 6: 10

Do you ever wonder why it feels so good inside when you help someone? It may be because you are obeying Jesus.

Jesus said that we should love each other as he loved us. Jesus helped people. At first he helped in his family. When he grew older he helped new people that he met. After he started his ministry, he traveled to other places to help people. He healed the sick, fed the hungry, and taught people to love God and each other.

Jesus left the riches of heaven to come to earth as a servant. He showed us, through his life, how we should live. He obeyed his Heavenly Father. His character was flawless. His heart was full of goodness and mercy to all of those who were truly seeking him.

Even when Jesus had a very busy ministry, he did not forget his family or his friends. He loved them too. He taught them through his words and actions. He sometimes had to correct them. He met their spiritual and physical needs. He prayed with them and for them. He forgave them. He had fellowship with them, sharing the good things of life. Jesus never forgot to show love to those closest to him and neither should we.

Dear Jesus, thank you for helping us and showing us how to help others.

"Come to me, all you who are weary and burdened, and I will give you rest."
Matthew 11:28

Rest

**In peace I will lie down and sleep, for you alone,
Lord, make me dwell in safety.**
Psalm 4:8

We are not machines. We need rest to be healthy and strong. When we don't get enough rest, we feel tired and grumpy. If we are very tired and do not rest, we can make mistakes which would cause harm to others and ourselves. God gave us one day a week to rest. He also gave us the night.

Night is a special "lights out" time for us to take the healing rest of sleep. Like recharging a battery, sleep refreshes us and gets us ready for another day.

Go to bed on time. Don't let work or play keep you up all night, and don't worry about problems. No one ever solved problems by worrying about them.

Pray before going to sleep. Give your problems to God who is big enough to take care of them. Some of the most difficult problems are solved after prayer and a good night's sleep.

*Thank you, Jesus, for the spiritual and physical
rest you give to those who trust in you.*

"Peace I leave with you; my peace I give you."
John 14:27a

Fear Not

"Do not let your hearts be troubled and do not be afraid."
John 14:27c

Are you afraid of the dark? Are you afraid of scary monsters? Are you afraid of storms?

Fear of the unknown can make children and adults feel afraid. If you believe in Jesus, you should not live in fear. You can snuggle up with a Bible promise. Romans 8:39 tells us that nothing will be able to separate us from the love of God that is in Christ Jesus our Lord.

If you feel afraid, pray and ask for God's peace and protection. Think about how much God the Father loves you. Remember that Jesus died to save you, and the Holy Spirit is there to comfort you. Pray and sing songs about God's goodness and his love.

Faith and fear cannot live together. When we are filled with the love of God, there is no room for fear. In his light, there is no darkness.

Thank you, God, that you are near.

"Let the little children come to me, and do not hinder them, for the kingdom of God belongs to such as these."
Mark 10:14

Jesus Welcomed Children

Yet to all who did receive him, to those who believed in his name, he gave the right to become children of God—

John 1:12

When God the Son walked the earth as a man, he showed great power. He calmed the storm, fed the hungry, healed the sick, cast out evil spirits, raised the dead, and changed the lives of sinners. These are just a few of the great things he did for those who believed in him. The crowds were amazed by his miracles.

One day when Jesus was very busy helping people, some parents brought their children to him. His disciples, knowing how important Jesus was, tried to turn the children away. But Jesus told the disciples to let the little children come to him, and then he blessed them.

We are never too young or too old to believe in Jesus. We are never too young or too old to learn from him. All who truly seek him will find him. He will never turn anyone away.

Dear Jesus, thank you for coming to Earth to be our Savior and Lord. Help even little ones trust in you.

"For God did not send his Son into the world to condemn the world, but to save the world through him."
John 3:17

Dear Jesus,
I believe that you died for me. I believe that you were
buried and rose from the grave to give me new life.
I accept you as my Savior and Lord.

Share Jesus With Others

. . . "Everyone who calls on the name of the Lord will be saved."

Romans 10:13

God the Father is very good and very loving, but he does not like sin. Sin is not trusting God. It is living life our own way instead of the way he tells us to live. The Bible says we have all sinned. We cannot be good enough to get to heaven on our own. We need a Savior.

Jesus, the Son of God, willingly agreed to come to earth to be born of a virgin. He was the Messiah, the one promised by the prophets to save people from their sins. His birth was anounced by angels to shepherds. He was visited by wise men. In the temple, he astounded his teachers with his wisdom. He performed miracles. Then he was taken by Roman soldiers to a cross where he died according to the Heavenly Father's plan. Jesus was the perfect Lamb of God who died for the sins of the world. Three days after he was buried, Jesus rose from the grave to prove that he was the Son of God, our Redeemer Messiah.

God is called by many names, but there is only one name that we can call on to save us, the name of Jesus. Have you ever asked Jesus to save you? If you have not, call on him now.

The Testimony of Jesus

Some of the things Jesus said about himself,
taken from the Gospel of John.

6:29b

Jesus answered, "The work of God is this:
to believe in the one he has sent."

6:51a-b

"I am the living bread that came down
from heaven. Whoever eats this bread
will live forever."

8:12	When Jesus spoke again to the people, he said, "I am the light of the world. Whoever follows me will never walk in darkness, but will have the light of life."
10:9	"I am the gate; whoever enters through me will be saved. They will come in and go out, and find pasture."
10:10b	"I have come that they may have life, and have it to the full."
10:11	"I am the good shepherd. The good shepherd lays down his life for the sheep."
10:27	"My sheep listen to my voice; I know them, and they follow me."
10:28	"I give them eternal life, and they shall never perish; no one will snatch them out of my hand."
10:30	"I and the Father are one."
11:25a	Jesus said to her, "I am the resurrection and the life."
11:26	"And whoever lives by believing in me will never die. Do you believe this?"

"You are the salt of the earth."
Matthew 5:13a

Be Salt

**Let your conversation be always full of grace,
seasoned with salt,
so that you may know how to answer everyone.**
Colossians 4:6

Afer Jesus had blessed people in his Sermon on the Mount, Jesus called his followers the salt of the earth. When Jesus spoke of salt, the people understood that salt was a preservative. The people knew it was used to keep meat from decaying. It could also be used as a seasoning to make food taste better.

We need to be salt, too. Living out our Christian faith is a benefit to everyone. It preserves our world. It is an encouragement to other believers. It is a witness to those who want to know Christ. Even the little things that we say or do can help preserve goodness. Even our little grains of salt can bring happiness, hope, and enjoyment to a sometimes tasteless world.

Help us to be salt, even in difficult situations. Help us to speak wise words that will honor you, and bring healing and encouragement to others.

"You are the light of the world."
Matthew 5:14 a

Let Your Light Shine

"In the same way, let your light shine before others, that they may see your good deeds and glorify your Father in heaven."
Matthew 5:16

In the Sermon On The Mount, Jesus said his followers were the light of the world. What did Jesus mean by these words?

Jesus was the great light that came to earth over two thousand years ago. He came to show people what the Heavenly Father was really like. He came to reveal truth. He came to show mercy. He came to seek and save those who were lost. He came to take our sins away. He came to light the way to a better, more abundant life.

Jesus wants his followers to be lights too. We shine for Jesus by discovering the things that he puts in our hearts to do, and doing those things for his glory. He does not want his people to bury their talents, but to shine the light of God's love into the dark places of life. He wants his "little lights" to show lonely, hurting people how God can heal and restore what the enemy has taken away. He wants his "little lights" to be a witness for him by how we live, what we say, and what we do.

Thank you for the people you bring into our lives that help us to share your "good news" with the world.

"For God so loved the world that he gave his one and only Son,
that whoever believes in him shall not perish but have eternal life."
John 3:16

What Is Heaven Like?

"And if I go and prepare a place for you, I will come back and take you to be with me that you also may be where I am going."
John 14:3

Have you accepted Jesus as your Savior? If you have, you have a great future ahead of you.

Heaven is a beautiful new creation with riches beyond compare. It is referenced several places in the Bible. A great place to learn about it is in Revelations 21 and 22.

In heaven everyone will have a better body. No one will get sick or die. No one will have sorrow or pain. There will be no tears for God will have wiped them away forever.

We will not be afraid in our beautiful new home for there is nothing that can harm us. Even the animals that were wild on earth will not hurt us or each other in this friendly place.

We will have a great time of fellowship in heaven. There will be great food, good music and glorious praise songs. Our loved ones and our friends who believed in Jesus will be there. We will see famous people that we have read about in books. We will meet other people from different lands and cultures. We will have plenty of time to talk to everyone.

What will be our happiest time in heaven? I believe it will be when we see Jesus our Savior, face to face.

"Blessed are the pure in heart for they will see God."
Matthew 5:8

Printed in the United States
By Bookmasters